100

THINGS TO DO IN
SACRAMENTO
BEFORE YOU
DIE

D1617420

100

THINGS TO DO IN
SACRAMENTO
BEFORE YOU
DIE

• •

MARK S. ALLEN

REEDY PRESS

Library of Congress Control Number: 2016946124

ISBN: 9781681060613

Design by Jill Halpin

Printed in the United States of America
16 17 18 19 20 5 4 3 2 1

Please note that websites, phone numbers, addresses, and company names are subject to change or cancellation. We did our best to relay the most accurate information available, but due to circumstances beyond our control, please do not hold us liable for misinformation. When exploring new destinations, please do your homework before you go.

DEDICATION

Thank you to my first boss John Clay who taught me that a broadcast market is first and foremost a community and to give back to that community relentlessly. He also helped me edit the first draft of this book and likely spell corrected many words, like relentlessly.

Thank you to my family and Sacramento for giving me a life that has exceeded my dreams!

CONTENTS

• •

● ●

Sports and Recreation

• •

Shopping and Fashion

FOREWORD

First and foremost, I hope you're not in any hurry—if you know what I'm saying. If you are, thankfully your bucket list is right here and ready, but I'd skip this foreword if I were you!

I've lived in Sacramento most of my life and have compiled over twenty-five-thousand hours of live television, discovering, testing, and tasting these places, and I assure you I'll have my knees broken by some executive chef whose multi-starred restaurant I've somehow left out of the list. Narrowing, not expanding, the list was the hardest part. Next door to almost each awesome place on these pages is an equally awesome place that I had to cut to get down to one hundred.

When I first moved to Sacramento, the standard, flippant response to "What is there to do in Sacramento?" was "One, go to San Francisco, two, go to Tahoe," etc. However, in this millennium, Sacramento has evolved into a history-filled, culturally explosive, world-class destination and one of California's must-visit places. *Time* magazine recently headlined, "Sacramento Is the Most Integrated and Culturally Diverse City in America." You're about to find out why.

Perhaps you were given this book as a Welcome Wagon gift, or maybe you're a local who needs a reminder of all the great things you've been meaning to do. Either way, I think it will come in handy. I've tried to balance among expensive and free, and have taken a TMZ approach: Sacramento proper gets first billing; anything exceptional in the "thirty-mile zone" from city center was considered!

Have fun, and be sure to join other readers on Facebook at 100ThingsSac to report your discoveries!

FOOD AND DRINK

EAT
IN THE KITCHEN

Imagine your friend is one of the world's best chefs, his friend is
one of Northern California's leading sommeliers—they're super
friendly and funny, and they invite you over for wine tasting and a
four-hour feast! That's what it's like at The Kitchen, where the food
is amazing and plentiful and you'll want for nothing. A bit pricey,
about two hundred dollars per person, but this is a special occasion,
right? I put it first because if you make reservations now, you may
get to this by the time you finish the others on the list (seriously, plan
at least five months ahead). This was my first meal when I moved
to Northern California, as a treat from my new employer; my next
meal was two-for-ninety-nine-cents tacos. Back to you—do this. It
is a bucket-list-worthy foodgasm!

2225 Hurley Way, 916-568-7171
thekitchenrestaurant.com

TIP

The menu is prix-fixe, and you'll get your money's worth, but add on the wine pairing; you'll save bucks. Also get ready to be tempted to sample some very, VERY expensive sakes and whiskeys. If you so indulge, do.

TRY
THE NEW iTACO!

Let me explain: I've never met a taco I didn't like. However, Chando's Tacos are not only the absolute best street tacos I have ever experienced, but they also are the only street tacos created by a former Apple Inc. executive. Lisandro "Chando" Madrigal left the iPhone mothership and within six years had his NorCal taco empire established. Chando discovered his love of tacos on a family trip to Mexico when he was a kid, where beneath the neon lights and busy streets in Tijuana, he saw white taco carts on nearly every corner. Though there are several versions of this taco-stand-turned-sit-down (including the new ten-thousand-square-foot restaurant/operations center in West Sacramento), you really should head to the one that started it all.

863 Arden Way, 916-641-8226
chandostacos.com

3

LIVE
THE AMERICAN DREAM (ROLL)

You'll find it at Mikuni's, and if you are lucky, your life will be transformed as you meet owner/chef Taro Arai. At the tender age of eleven, Taro saved $6,000 from a paper route to move his family from Japan to Sacramento, where not long after, they created this gem. The rolls are all original and amazing. The fusion sushi is an East meets West Coast meets East Coast meets Taro. Case in point: the 24k roll contains real twenty-four-karat gold and is aptly priced. There are plenty of locations around the Sacramento area, even one near Lake Tahoe skiing in Truckee, and you can enjoy Mikuni's at a Kings game in Golden 1 Center. Check the website for special events and classes, including public or private sushiology lessons!

1530 J St., 916-447-2112
mikunisushi.com

5

MIDNIGHT
MILKSHAKES!

Rick's Dessert Diner is great at all hours, but even better after spilling out of a show, concert, or club downtown. Award-winning milkshakes and cakes and pies come with a price: you will stand in a line with customers "anxious to get their carb on," but otherwise very nice people just like you. Rick's Dessert Diner has more than 285 varieties of European and American desserts, all made fresh daily from scratch, using generations-old recipes originating in France, Italy, Germany, Sweden, Switzerland, and even early America. And Rick's custom cakes for birthdays, anniversaries, weddings, and showers are works of art! I challenge you to peruse their menu without your mouth watering. Voted "Best of Sacramento" for dessert every year since 1986!

2401 J St., 916-444-0969
ricksdessertdiner.com

ROCK
YOUR PIZZA

The moment you walk into Pizza Rock and see a giant semi-truck crashing through the ceiling, you know this is not your average pizza joint. Tony Gemignani knows pizza; he is a twelve-time World Pizza Champion. Everything on the menu here is a bit exceptional and elevated. The pizzas are gourmet, the handcrafted cocktails are artisan, and the pastas, calzones, stromboli, antipasti, and salads are all made from authentic Italian ingredients and organically grown produce. Tony Soprano would love this place! And although Pizza Rock is a restaurant first and foremost, it's about more than just food—customers are also drawn to the electric energy inside this space. Even Sunday brunch here is energized; this is not your traditional pizzeria. They do deliver, but don't be silly—you need to experience this!

1020 K St., 916-737-5777
pizzarocksacramento.com

CELEBRATE
OCTOBERFEST 365!

But at Der Biergarten, they'll ask you to spell it "Oktoberfest."
Der Biergarten is a beer lover's dream come true. It's authentically
German with an extensive beer selection and a light German food
menu, including thirty-two beers on draft and sausages brought
in fresh from Sacramento's number-one German butcher. Even
its tables were shipped to Sacramento from relatives in Germany,
and you will be seated in a communal atmosphere, sipping great
German beer from half- and full-liter steins. The experience is one
hundred percent outdoors, so you can enjoy the great Sacramento
weather by day and the stars by night. Make sure you plan to stay a
while, and plan a safe ride home. While you came to eat and drink,
you'll likely be challenged to a game of corn hole, Foosball, or
ping-pong. Lederhosen are optional, although I've never really
seen any there.

2332 K St., 916-346-4572
beergardensacramento.com

SACRAMENTO'S MICROBREWS ABOUND! HERE ARE THE MUST-SIPS

Ruhstaller

Founded by Captain Frank Ruhstaller, "California's Premier Pioneer Brewer," more than 130 years ago. The good captain grew the finest hops and barley by partnering with California farmers.

630 K St., 916-447-1881
ruhstallerbeer.com

Oak Park Brewing Company

Set in a lovely ninety-year-old building that makes you feel like you're on a luxurious rustic ship—and they have extraordinary beer! There are usually seven beers on tap, and each one always seems to be from a different planet than the one beside it. Their British and Belgian ales have often been described as having a "West Coast kick," and their IPAs are known for being aromatic and hoppy, with a smooth malt finish.

3514 Broadway, 916-660-2723
opbrewco.com

TIP

Come here to buy a "growler" and to find out what that actually is!

Rubicon Brewing Company

A two-time Gold Medalist at the Great American Beer Festival, Rubicon Brewing Company is the longest-running brewery in the Sacramento area, established in 1987. According to their website, "of the 1,679 brewers in operation today, only seventy-four were around in 1990," and Rubicon was one of those seventy-four!

2004 Capitol Ave., 916-448-7032
rubiconbrewing.com

EAT VIP

Every city has "that" restaurant where old money meets new money meets the most special of occasions that prompted dining at one of the most expensive and historic restaurants in town. The Firehouse is just that in Sacramento. Ronald Reagan had his inaugural dinner here, and The Firehouse has hosted every California governor since. Paul McCartney and a list of A-listers far too long for this book have chosen this venue for their Sacramento dining. Try to talk your waiter into a tour of the wine cellar, where Andy Warhol once perused the twenty thousand bottles to choose from while eating a cheeseburger with Mario the sommelier!

1112 2nd St., 916-442-4772
firehouseoldsac.com

YO, MOFO!

When the food truck explosion was sweeping the nation, Sacramento's finest trucks gathered for a cooperative summit, and SactoMoFo (Sacramento Mobile Food Events) was born! Drewski's Hot Rod Kitchen is the most uniquely Sacramento, with the most amazing pulled pork sandwiches I've had anywhere in the world. Bacon Mania is a truck that serves dishes that are all about the bacon, including crisps, sandwiches, fries, and cheese & mac. It's Nacho Truck has taken cheese on chips to an art form; just remember their slogan—"It's Nacho Truck . . . It's Mine!" SactoMoFo's list is long and proud. Catch the list for these and more than thirty other once-in-a-lifetime-experience food trucks at their site; check for location and dates.

SactoMoFo
sactomofo.com

PINCH A TAIL
AND SUCK A HEAD

That is a perfectly family-friendly play-by-play tutorial on how to eat crayfish, and that's exactly what's on the menu at Crawdads on the River. Sacramento is a river city, after all, and many a worthy eatery lines the banks. However, this is one that will put you on the river and into the action. Adam Pechal and Paul Caravelli, both from ABC's *The Taste*, teamed to resurrect this floating dining, drinking, party barge-meets-refined living. Make reservations to be outside on a nice day, and Louisiana-inspired anything on the menu will meet high expectations. Make friends with the people next to you who own the million-dollar yacht they've just docked, and your night may get more interesting!

1375 Garden Highway, 916-929-2268
saccrawdads.com

FOX AND GOOSE
FOR BREAKFAST!

Neither is on the menu here at the historic Fox and Goose Public House, but now that I have your attention, DO NOT MISS THIS PLACE! It was established in 1975, but the bones of the building date back to 1913, and it is a descendant of the original Fox and Goose in West Yorkshire, England, that has been open for more than two hundred years. It's a rare day that you're not dining next to someone from the United Kingdom, as subjects of the royals are drawn here for a taste of home. While the English breakfasts are authentic, everything on the menu excels. They mix coffee drinks and cocktails with equal fervor, and it's typically pint-o'clock at any hour. Enjoy live music on weekends and some weeknights; the line can get long, but it's worth the wait.

1001 R St., 916-443-8825
foxandgoose.com

BECOME A BIKER...
A BREW-BIKER

Book a seat on the Sac Brew Bike, then sip and pedal your way through the Downtown/Midtown area. Imagine a bicycle built for two, but make that built for fifteen, where everyone uses pedaling power to move this music-blasting round table of fun. You'll also stop at pubs to take a break from the pedaling, but not the beering. Whether you take the standard Brew & Pub two-hour, the extended three-hour, or the special Pedal to Plate tour, you're going to have a blast cruising this "partybike" at a blazing five miles per hour. Never fear . . . you'll have a safe driver behind the Sac Brew Bike wheel. But make sure you have a safe ride home; you'll be too tired to drive if nothing else!

1519 19th St., 916-952-7973
sacbrewbike.com

FINAL DESTINATION:
HO HOS

Let me explain. Sacramento's RT (Regional Transit) light rail is one of the most efficient public transportation systems of its size in the nation, and even more popular since the Golden 1 Center made it the best way to get in and out of downtown. So now that you're using it, take advantage of its path to one of the most amazing bakery cafes you'll ever know. Take the light rail to Folsom, stay on to the very last stop, and it will put you right at Karen's Bakery. Be prepared for a line wrapped around the block on weekends, but the wait will be well worth it.

Everything baked is exceptional, and you'll find artisan touches in every item on the breakfast and lunch menus. Be sure to save room for dessert, and I highly recommend the handcrafted Ho Hos . . . they're the best I've ever had. A disclaimer: they're the *only* handcrafted Ho Hos I've ever had. But regardless, I dream of them often now. What else? The Ho Hos! You just gotta try one yourself . . . dipped in chocolate ganache, with creamy rum filling. They actually are intoxicating; it's a good thing you're not driving.

705 Gold Lake Dr., Folsom, 916-985-2665
karensbakery.com

SQUEEZE IN TO
SQUEEZE INN

Long before Guy Fieri featured this burger joint on *Diners, Drive-Ins and Dives*, this godsend to the craft burger scene had a crowd from open to close. Although several other locations have opened, you may want to journey to the original to say that you did. It's a bit on the small side, best described as half a shack. And you will, no matter your girth, find yourself squeezing in to find your fit at the bar or a table. Get ready for the best cheeseburger you've ever had: order the Squeezeburger with Cheese, and you'll thank me later. The cheese will ooze out upon the grill and be crisped upon delivery. The West Sacramento, Roseville, and downtown Sacramento locations also have ample non-squeeze room, but the same culinary burger technology is in play.

5301 Power Inn Rd., 916-386-8599
thesqueezeinn.com

PARADISE PICNIC

There are several great spots to picnic throughout the Sacramento area, but I've picked one because you're running out of time. Selland's Market Cafe was created by Randall Selland, who knows a thing or two about great food; he has opened and maintains several award-winning restaurants in the region. Stop at Selland's to pick up supplies to create your own picnic, or get their pre-made picnic components for a perfect meal. I lived in NYC and discovered the internationally famous Dean & DeLuca. But Selland's is their equal and perhaps ups them in the organic, sustainable, farm-fresh way. Now that you're picnicked up, head to Paradise Beach only one-quarter mile away, and have the best beach dining experience in town. There are three Selland's to choose from, but only this one fits the masterful picnic plan.

5340 H St., 916-736-3333
sellands.com

Paradise Beach, 5211 Carlson Dr.

HAVE A 50-50
AT GUNTHER'S

Sacramento has five unique and must-try creameries, but Gunther's Ice Cream Shop wins, since it was the first. Little has changed since it opened way back in 1940. Gunther's ice cream is still made fresh and with the original recipes. They also make one hundred fruit freezes, and before you become room temperature, you MUST try the Frozen 50-50. It's a scoop of vanilla on top of the fruit freeze of your choice. As it melts, the flavors comingle into perfection.

2801 Franklin Blvd., 916-457-6646
gunthersicecream.com

SACRAMENTO HAS A LONG TRADITION OF FINE FAMILY CREAMERIES WAITING TO FREEZE YOUR BRAIN. HERE ARE TWO MORE.

Leatherby's Family Creamery

Family run . . . throw a maraschino cherry and you'll likely hit a Leatherby in this place. Come for the sundaes, but the crab sandwich is shockingly amazing for an ice cream place!

2333 Arden Way, 916-920-8382
leatherbys.net

Vic's Ice Cream

Also a blast from the past straight out of 1947 (the year it opened), with vintage décor and vintage comfort menu. Besides ice cream, try the wonderful sandwiches, cakes, pies, and bonbons.

3199 Riverside Blvd., 916-448-0892
vicsicecream.com

DINE
ON A BRIDGE!

Sacramento is officially the nation's farm-to-fork capital, and the best way to experience local food from local farms is also the hardest ticket in town to get. Once a year, our own "Golden Gate Bridge," the Tower Bridge (to West Sacramento), is closed to traffic and transformed into the Farm-to-Fork Gala Dinner, part of the Farm-to-Fork Taste of Summer festivities. This family-style feast features the most award-winning food and wine in the region, all prepared by local chefs, offering locally grown and artisanally prepared ingredients. You almost have to know someone, or know someone who knows someone, to get in. And if you do manage to get a pair of tickets to this extravaganza, since we now know each other (by virtue of you buying this book), I'll gladly accept your invitation to be your "plus one"! Go to their website now in hopes of getting on the list for next year . . . tickets go that fast.

On the Sacramento Tower Bridge, 916-808-7777
farmtofork.com

BE A SULTAN
AT CASABLANCA!

Even if you don't order the Sultan Feast at Casablanca Moroccan Restaurant (but I suggest that you do—after all this is a bucket list), you will feel like royalty! Mourhit Drissi is the owner and will make you family during your first moments here. He will help guide you through the intricacies of the meal you're about to enjoy, all still cooked from ancient traditions passed down to his family. And Mourhit will enhance the experience with anecdotal references to each dish's Moroccan origin. The atmosphere is awesome and so much fun for big groups. You'll sit on cushions and eat almost everything only with your hands. Be warned, it's located in a less-than-attractive strip mall, ugly even by strip mall standards; however, inside, Casablanca equals Xanadu!

3516 Fair Oaks Blvd., 916-979-1160

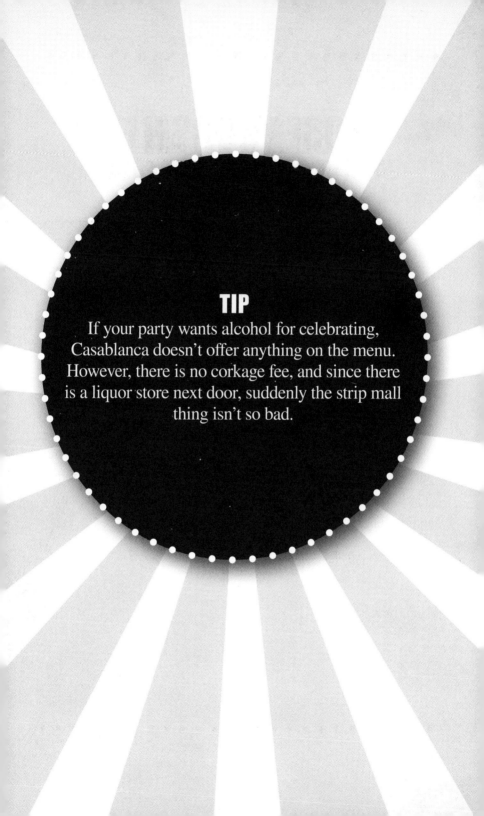

TIP

If your party wants alcohol for celebrating, Casablanca doesn't offer anything on the menu. However, there is no corkage fee, and since there is a liquor store next door, suddenly the strip mall thing isn't so bad.

LOSE YOURSELF
IN THE COACHELLA OF FOOD AND BEVERAGE!

Part of the annual Farm-to-Fork Taste of Summer festivities is the Farm-to-Fork Festival, a one-day event that takes over ten blocks of downtown Sacramento's Capitol Mall. An aerial photograph of the miles of people leading to the Capitol looks like an inaugural celebration is taking place! Designed to showcase and celebrate where our food and drinks come from, the Farm-to-Fork Festival brings us face to face with the people who are feeding our region and the world. This free festival boasts a delicious selection of farm-to-fork offerings that are produced and available in the Sacramento region. You'll find food, wine, and beer from regional eateries and purveyors, as well as live music, five live cooking demonstration stages, a kids' zone, interactive booths from local grocers, farms and ranches, and more!

On the Sacramento Capitol Mall, 916-808-7777
farmtofork.com

PICNIC UNDERGROUND

Sorry to "Sacramento's best-kept secret," but I'm putting it in the book. The Underground Wine Tasting Room presents quite possibly one of the most romantic and charming nights you can find in this town, especially at this price point. You'll travel down steps, underground to the original street level of Sacramento, and be surrounded by bottles emblazoned with logos of Twisted Twig and Rendez-Vous wineries, among others. You'll lounge at bistro-style tables in the brick courtyard, enjoying an atmosphere reminiscent of quaint rural towns in France. Cheese plates, succulent chocolates, and more complement the tastings and/or stand on their own. You need to do this!

900 2nd St., Original Level, 916-444-2349
theundergroundtastingroom.com

UP YOUR MOXIE

Think NYC's Little Italy meets California fresh, and that's Moxie. How often do you see this on a menu: *"At Moxie, you get what you want. If it's in the building, or nearby, we will prepare it!"* And they mean it. Notice the Cary Grant photo on the wall in this dimly lit, deeper than wide room. Perhaps you are in NYC! Adam, the owner, will greet you upon entering and will take you every step of the way to make sure your night is special. If he senses you want to be alone, he'll give you room. If you're social, he may sit, open a bottle of wine and share it with you. "Special" is an understatement when describing this place. Moxie is a must. There are more daily specials than there are regular items on the menu!

2028 H St., 916-443-7585
moxierestaurant.com

HAVE A MOJITO
WITH A MERMAID

Although I've traveled around the world, I've never seen anything quite like this. At Dive Bar, a giant overhead aquarium runs the entire length of the bar. And in that aquarium . . . MERMAIDS! REAL MERMAIDS!! Okay, they *might as well be* real mermaids. Actresses/performance artists, wearing the most convincing Hollywood special effects prosthetic tails, free dive nightly and mermaid about as you sip and mingle. We took turns timing the mermaids, convinced that some of them might be the real deal, since humans can't hold their breath that long. Despite the name Dive Bar, it really is a nice bar and occasionally offers live music on the weekends. Regardless, you're here for the mermaids. A truly unique must-see!

1016 K St., 916-737-5999
divebarsacramento.com

PATIO IT
AT PARAGARY'S

The moment you enter this open-air courtyard, you'll know you're in the right place for a special time. This bistro's airy environment opens up to a renowned patio where you can dine surrounded by waterfalls, sixty-year-old olive trees, and a giant fireplace. Randy Paragary is a Sacramento restaurant pioneer and is among the few who can claim early rights to the trademark of "California cuisine." Paragary's is tried and true and quite special for anytime. If this is your first time or only time in California, after eating here, you'll know you've had signature dishes at their best.

1403 28th St., 916-452-3335
paragarys.com

SAVE YOUR MONEY
FOR THE POUR HOUSE

Actually, save your money for a safe ride home, because at the Pour House . . . *you pour your own beer and whiskey!* Yes! Right at your table! You'll have nice beers to choose from at your fingertips, and Jameson is on tap. If you're more into high-end libations, they have them as well; Pour House actually offers an amazing variety of spirits, beers, and wines. The food menu is upscale gastropub style, featuring local produce, natural meats, and sustainable seafood. And, please—eat. You may be sorry if you don't, for a multitude of reasons!

910 Q St., 916-706-2465
pourhousesacramento.com

SPEND A VERY HAPPY HOUR
WITH THE SHADY LADY

Esquire magazine named it "one of the top bars in America," and for good reason. At The Shady Lady Saloon, they do the classics right, and while taking your order, the mixologist will get to know you to make sure your drink not only meets your expectations but exceeds them. I personally don't drink, but I have been along on many Shady Lady outings, and it is one of the best vibes in town for brunch, lunch, or dinner. Speaking of food, Shady Lady offers the best charcuterie in NorCal. For this featured menu item, Chef chooses the day's best local artisanal and housemade meats and cheeses, Acme sourdough baguette, cured olives, pork rinds (handmade!), and more. Take that, bar food!

1409 R St., 916-231-9121
shadyladybar.com

EAT
AT CALIFORNIA'S OTHER LEGISLATIVE HOUSE

Way back in 1939, Frank Fat turned a former speakeasy into what would become the kitchen table to some of the most prominent lawmakers in America. The California State Capitol is only a block away, and Frank Fat's restaurant is where landmark bills were and continue to be negotiated over friendly meals and napkin deals by hungry legislators. Frank Fat's features traditional but elevated Chinese food, with recipes originating in China's Peking, Szechuan, Canton, and Shanghai provinces, as well as Hong Kong. But a strong hint of its speakeasy roots remains, with American dishes available as well. Glance around during your meal, and if anyone looks like a politician here, they probably are! Be sure to discreetly eavesdrop to hear tomorrow's news!

806 L St., 916-442-7092
fatsrestaurants.com

GO
TO COFFEE CHURCH

At Temple Coffee Roasters, you can walk in and order the best coffee or espresso drink you've ever had, OR you can actually learn the art of espresso or coffee roasting and extracting in one of the many classes the company offers. It sounds intimidating, but it's actually fascinating and infinitely more fun than you'd expect. The syllabus says, *"Covers the fundamental variables that affect coffee extraction quality including coffee-to-water ratio, agitation and more!"* You'll leave enlightened, and you will be the coffee master of your domain. Multiple locations; Midtown is my favorite.

2829 S St., 916-454-1272
templecoffee.com

JOIN
THE GRANGE!

Or don't. I just needed a headline! The Grange was a farmers' association organized in 1867, and this restaurant of the same name might as well have been its headquarters. Much has been said of Sacramento being the genesis of "farm to fork," and no executive chef has embraced the concept more than Oliver Ridgeway at Grange. I challenge any chef anywhere in the world to produce a better pork chop. When asked how they're prepared, I was told: "It's brined in apple cider, vinegar, cloves, cinnamon, chili flakes, and whole oranges. The meat, submerged and chilled for twenty-four to thirty-six hours, absorbs the liquid and plumps." WOW! And that's just the pork chop. The service, architecture, and ambiance of this restaurant is definitive Sacramento at its best.

926 J St., 916-492-4450
grangesacramento.com

MUSIC AND ENTERTAINMENT

LIVE THE MOVIE

IMAX Corporation will tell you that any IMAX experience is a great experience. However, having been to the nation's top twenty-five IMAX locations, I can tell you that, with the exception of the Smithsonian Museum's IMAX, Sacramento's Esquire IMAX Theatre is the best immersion movie presentation you'll find. Originally a 1930s movie palace, and then many other things before returning to its theater glory, Esquire IMAX offers upscale food, beer, and wine. You'll recline comfortably in one of the 388 leather rocker seats while viewing IMAX's largest, six-story high, eighty-foot-wide screen, with 18,000 watts of digital wraparound sound. Prince, rest in peace, had this on his list: in 2014 he rented the entire theater for a private date.

1211 K St., 916-443-4629
imax.com/imax-esquire-oo

DIE ON THE DELTA KING, BEFORE YOU DIE

Well, let's hope it's not you who gets offed at The Delta King Murder Mystery! This is a great night out for a multitude of reasons. It's located onboard a historic moored riverboat, and that's cool in itself. Your evening begins with a very nice dinner party in the original dining quarters of the ship. Then, without warning, someone gets whacked! You'll spend the rest of the evening trying to solve the murder mystery. This is great for a date or a group of up to 250! Highly recommended: the package in which you'll spend the night onboard in a stateroom and be treated to an amazing breakfast in the morning. The best bacon I've had in NorCal was on this boat. If someone had to die for great bacon, so be it!

1000 Front St., 916-444-5464
deltaking.com

COMEDY SPOT

100 THINGS TO DO IN
SAC BEFORE YOU DIE

WWW.SACCOMEDYSPOT.COM

SPOT THE COMEDY

Comedy Spot owner Brian Crall said, "I don't just want an improv club good enough for Sacramento, I want a club that would blow the doors off of any club in the world." And he accomplished that early on. You'll not find a funnier night of comedy than the prime-time, nine p.m., Saturday night performance featuring his varsity troupe, the Anti-Cooperation League. The troupe has launched many a network career and routinely has drop-in guests from *Parks and Recreation* and *Kids in the Hall*, as well as Officer Byrd of *Judge Judy* fame. All shows here are good; ACL is exceptional!

1050 20th St., #130, 916-444-3137
saccomedyspot.com

ACE A CONCERT

Ace of Spades, although relatively new on the Sacramento live music scene, is a great place to see an act that would usually sell out a much larger venue. There are four bars, although most often the shows are all-ages, and there is a family-friendly area with great food. Warning—plan for a late night, as the acts don't always hit the stage on time. Once I was there to enjoy a Snoop Dog show that was scheduled to start at 7:30 p.m.; he didn't take the stage until eleven. Wait . . . that probably was Snoop Dog just being Snoop Dog. Either way, check the schedule often for a diverse and impressive list of indie rock, pop, and hip-hop artists.

1417 R St., 916-930-9220
aceofspadessac.com

SACRAMENTO HAS SEVERAL TRIED-AND-TRUE LIVE MUSIC VENUES. ALSO CHECK OUT:

Old Ironsides

Old Ironsides has been jammin' since 1934. In fact, it received Sacramento's very first liquor license when Prohibition ended (although rumor has it that Prohibition didn't exactly slow their roll). Since that time, Old Ironsides has been offering up great music at a great price, anywhere from free to five dollars, plus food and beverage specials to match. Many Sacramento-turned-famous bands have rolled through here, including Cake and Papa Roach.

1901 10th St., 916-443-9751
theoldironsides.com

Harlow's Restaurant & Nightclub

This is as close to an old-fashioned supper club as you're going to get. Harlow's has a great dinner show, often followed by two later shows, featuring the best in blues, jazz, rock, and pop. Since 1982, this is where true music lovers go, and where musicians go to hear live music. Harlow's itself gets national acts, but don't be surprised to see the likes of Bruno Mars, after a sold-out arena show, chilling here to a live performance from the likes of one-time Prince protégé Andy Allo (yes, it happened).

2708 J St., 916-441-4693
harlows.com

Blue Lamp

This is a favorite old stand-by and the most diverse of the bunch. Expect a great vibe and great service, plus regional and national talent, including blues, rock, jazz, alternative, country, folk, DJ, and more. If you love music, Blue Lamp has something for you every night.

1400 Alhambra, 916-455-3400
bluelampsacramento.com

WATCH STRAY CATS
IN OLD SACRAMENTO

Or see other top jazz, blues, and pop performances during the weekend-long celebration at the Sacramento Music Festival. Every Memorial Day weekend since 1974, Old Sacramento and other downtown venues have been home to one of the area's biggest parties of the year. Originally called the Old Sacramento Dixieland Jazz Jubilee, the event has evolved with the changing times to include other styles of music in addition to classic jazz and swing. Despite the broadening of the musical scope, I hope you like to party, because this weekend continues have a Mardi Gras feel!

At various Old Sacramento venues, 916-444-2004
sacmusicfest.com

EXPERIENCE
THE MUSIC CIRCUS

When I first moved to Northern California, I was led hand in hand to an out-of-place full-sized circus tent on a hot summer day, oddly located in the middle of downtown. Once inside The Music Circus, I witnessed the best performance of *Cabaret* I've ever seen and lost thirty pounds in water weight from all the sweat; it was one hundred degrees, and it's hard to air-condition a circus tent. The good news is that by the twenty-first century, the tent was replaced by a permanent, air-conditioned structure that is still tent-like on the inside.

1510 J St., 916-557-1999
californiamusicaltheatre.com

DON'T
BE A SCROOGE

Any traces of your inner Scrooge will disappear if you go see Macy's Theater of Lights on Front and K Streets. Words can't describe how magical, how world class, this event truly is. Each year, kicking off Thanksgiving Eve and running through New Year's night, this live action-meets-digital projection-meets-multimedia art transforms a city block into a winter wonderland stage. Mark Twain steps out onto a balcony (which is the real balcony of the *Union* newspaper, where at a point in time the real Mark Twain used to work) and assists in telling the story of "'Twas the Night Before Christmas." Live appearances from pretty much everyone in that story, each night featuring a different local celebrity, combine with digital mapping and special effects created exclusively by Skywalker Sound. If the narrator's voice sounds familiar, that's because it is Bill Farmer, the voice of Disney's Goofy.

K and Front Sts., Old Sacramento, 916-970-5226
oldsacramento.com

TIPS

Two shows each night, usually but not always at 6:15 and 7:45 (check schedule). Like a Disney Main Street Parade, curbside is valued real estate, so get there early. There's great holiday shopping for unique small gifts at Stage Nine and Evangeline's (and great places to warm up). The best spot to watch is right in the middle of the street at 102 K Street, where you'll see all the surprises on both sides, and since the big finish is the lighting of the official sixty-foot-tall tree, you'll have the best vista of both the show and the tree! Parking can be tricky; best bets are: Old Sacramento Garage (I & 2nd Streets), Tower Garage (Capitol & Neasham), and Macy's West Garage (3rd & L Streets).

BE
A COMEDY TEST AUDIENCE

Because Sacramento is such a demographic melting pot, it's often used by major corporations to test-market products to evaluate their effectiveness for the rest of America. Did you know the same is true for comedy? The secret's out! For decades comics have been sneaking into Sacramento to test their jokes on the eve of a *Tonight Show*, Kimmel, or Conan appearance to see if they're going to work on the national telecast. Two clubs offer exclusive stand-up. The more historic of the two is Laughs Unlimited, where Jerry Seinfeld worked out his act over twenty-seven appearances. Jay Leno and the late Garry Shandling and Robin Williams were also regulars when they were climbing the stand-up ranks. It was the unofficial bullpen for the Carson *Tonight Show* era and still attracts national acts to its historic Old Sac room. The modern mecca of late night comedy is Punchline, located in a most unlikely strip mall, upstairs next to a mattress store. Dave Chappell, Louis C.K., Mike E. Winfield, Amy Schumer, and a long list of others have and continue to make the journey up the steps, past the Serta Perfect Sleeper, and onto the stage.

Laughs Unlimited, 1207 Front St.
916-446-8128, laughsunlimited.com

Punchline, 2100 Arden Way
916-925-8500, punchlinesac.com

B IN A PLAY

The B Street Theater is one of the most intimate and respected acting venues in town. You'll feel like you are actually in the play, as the ninety-nine seats touch and sometimes surround the performance area in this smallish black-box-style house. Despite its small size, B Street is one of the nation's most respected professional theaters, started by award-winning television, film, and stage star Timothy Busfield and his equally talented brother Buck. Seeing a play here will not likely be a once-in-a-lifetime experience—you'll hunger for more and you will be back. Though no stranger to comedy, you're more likely to find intense drama here.

2711 B St., 916-443-5300
bstreettheatre.org

ROCK
THE PARK

For more than twenty-five years, Sacramento has offered the best free live music happy hour the state has to offer. Concerts in the Park happens every Friday at Cesar Chavez Park from five to nine p.m., featuring multiple live bands. Some you've heard of (like Cake, Tesla, and Deftones), some not so much, but they're all good! Food and beverage will cost you less than most festivals, and again, the concerts are FREE! For all ages! Some of Sacramento's best local DJs will be spinning between sets. Nearby garages take care of your car, or arrive via RT light rail (try using their online trip planner at SacRT.com). There are even free bike valet services offered by SABA (Sacramento Area Bicycle Advocates). Fridays during May, June, and July.

At Cesar Chavez Park, 910 I St., 916-442-8575
godowntownsac.com

TESLA AND TACOS

Although Sacramento's famous metal band, Tesla, did play at Swabbies on the River, these days you're more likely to find a Jimmy Buffet, Gwen Steffani, Lynyrd Skynyrd, Steely Dan, Van Halen, or AC/DC cover band, plus a great view of the Sacramento River as it lazily rolls by that few places can brag about. Grab something cold to drink, a signature Swabbies brisket taco, and enjoy the perfect outdoor concert picnic.

5871 Garden Highway, 916-920-8088
swabbies.com

SEE
THE PIANO MAN

Listen to Billy Joel's song, and try to find one lyric not ringing true at Henry's Lounge. A waitress practicing politics, a real estate novelist, and Davey who's still in the Navy . . . all likely part of the colorful cast of characters you'll find in this dive bar that tries to be nothing but a dive bar, perhaps with the exception of the piano man who plays for tips in a jar, and, like in the song, probably gets his drinks for free. On Tuesday nights, it's open mic, and anyone who can play a tune can perform for the crowd. Inexpensive, friendly, and fun. They don't have a website, and don't bother Googling them. Please ask the bartender what their "hashtag" is, and then run!

1117 9th St., 916-446-0739

DANCE,
IN THE POOL

For nightlife, Faces historically has the best music, fifteen bars, three dance floors (one is Sacramento's biggest), and an open heated pool that anyone can use year-round. It's loud, wild, and best enjoyed in groups. And, oh yeah, it's also Sacramento's oldest and most populated gay club. Perhaps I should have led with that. I found out after the fact myself. I thought it was a just a fitness club night out before I realized it was just "out" out. Regardless, you'll find people of every orientation, no judging, and a good time here. And leave your cell phone home just in case you have an unplanned pool dance.

2000 K St., 916-448-7798
faces.net

FIND
ACOUSTIC SANCTUARY

On weekend nights, the corner of 22nd and J in Midtown Sacramento belongs to Winko. This performance artist, this one-man band named Winko Ljizz, has a piano bar like no other. The Acoustic Sanctuary has four wheels, five stools, a one-couple dance floor, and a baby grand piano that seems to have been built into this van. Winko also has within his reach at all times dozens of musical instruments that he uses in sets consisting of "the hits of today and yesteryear." See this, and good luck trying to describe it to anyone!

2201 J St., 916-454-9463
acousticsanctuary.com

SURVIVE
THE ROCKIN' RODEO

You'll survive, but you'll be sore after a night at Stoney's Rockin' Rodeo. I'm a non-country city slicker, yet I feel transformed every time I leave this place. The staff and patrons are super-friendly, and it's infinitely more diverse than you'd expect. You will learn to line dance—OH, YES, YOU WILL—it's not so much mandatory as it is infectious. Cheap drinks, good food, and horrible parking, but trust me, you should Uber or Lyft in and out of this place for a multitude of reasons!

Country or not, you will spend most of your time dancing. And the dancing or the mechanical bull will leave your muscles remembering the great time you had for days!

1320 Del Paso Blvd., 916-927-6023
stoneyinn.com

VIP
KARAOKE

Oishii Sushi Bar and Heartbeat Karaoke might be the most upscale karaoke experience you've ever had, taking it to a whole new level. You get a private room (rooms for up to forty are available) and your own private karaoke system. Each room is super-comfortable with wraparound furniture, as though it was designed by a limousine company. Bar and food service is controlled via an electronic pad in each room, as is the extensive big-screen, big-sound karaoke! The sushi is above average, and the experience is very special occasion-worthy!

1000 K St., Ste. 200, 916-557-8088
oishiisushikaraoke.com

DON'T WAIT TO DRIVE IN
TO THE MOVIES!

Sacramento is home to one of America's eighteen remaining drive-in movie theaters, so before you die, see a movie on a drive-in screen before it dies! This is an unforgettable experience and a tribute to America's past. Family owned and operated since 1952, West Wind combines the old-school drive-in vibe with the latest technology, boasting the largest digital projectors available. And the audio is beamed straight to your car stereo! Pack your favorite tailgating supplies, get there before sunset, and toss a Frisbee or football around before the show. An extensive full food snack bar is at the center, and it's always a double feature of first run films! Re-enact the drive-in scenes from *Grease* or *Pee-wee's Big Adventure* while you wait! Please tweet and tag me if you actually do.

9616 Oates Dr., 916-363-6572
westwinddi.com

SPORTS AND RECREATION

SAY THAT YOU'VE BEEN
TO THE BEST BASKETBALL ARENA IN NORTH AMERICA

Taking in a Kings game or any event in Golden 1 Center will indeed be memorable. Inaugurated by rock royalty Sir Paul McCartney, G1 Center is "The Coliseum of the 21st Century," with advanced state-of-the-art technology in every aspect. G1 has the largest 4k indoor video screen in North America, roughly the size of the basketball court itself. HD screens are located at every possible angle, so you don't miss a moment from anywhere. The G1 app will let you order food and beverage right to your seat. This is the most connected arena in the world, with more than one thousand access points to the fastest-streaming net in existence; it can handle five hundred thousand Snapchat posts per second! Acoustics were designed by the same group that upgraded Royal Albert Hall. You'll have no trouble remembering your experience because it's likely on your Snapchat Story!

547 L St., 916-928-6900
golden1center.com

WATCH RIVER CATS
IN THEIR NATURAL HABITAT

That is, see Sacramento's minor league baseball team, the Sacramento River Cats, play major-league level ball in our beautiful $47 million stadium they call home! Baseball is America, and Raley Field showcases the sport at its finest. The park, although in West Sacramento, offers you the best view of Sacramento, and there's not a bad seat in the venue. For less than half of what you would pay for parking at a Giants game, you can see their minor league team, and the same major-league quality of play. Save even more by sitting in the grassy wraparound outfield and you'll feel like you're part of the game!

400 Ballpark Dr., West Sacramento, 916-371-4487
sacramentorivercats.com

SEE A
GOAAAAAAAAAAAAAAAAAAAAAAL LIVE!

Since 2014, Sacramento has been the proud home of the Republic FC professional soccer team. I'm honored to have been the inaugural announcer for their first game at Hughes Stadium, with a record crowd of more than twenty thousand fans. Those fans have proliferated, and if you've never seen a pro soccer game, Republic FC home games are world-class in play and energy. There's not a bad seat at Bonnie Field, home field for Republic FC.

1600 Exposition Blvd., 916-307-6100
sacrepublicfc.com

BE
THE PINBALL WIZARD!

You don't have to be old enough to get that musical reference, or to even know what pinball is to enjoy one of the most unique lounges of any city—The Coin-Op Game Room. You just have to be twenty-one or older to enjoy, and you WILL enjoy! In fact, I dare you not to have a good time there, surrounded by wall-to-wall classic video arcade games representing literally every era of gaming since Pong, along with the aforementioned grandfather to the video game—pinball. Great food, great mixologist cocktails, and even an outdoor patio, where giant Jenga and giant Connect Four games await your challenge. I travel all over the world for a living; not once have I seen the likes of this club. A must!

908 K St., 916-661-6983
coinopsac.com

LEARN TO BE
A PRO WAKEBOARDER
WITHOUT A BOAT!

Wake Island Waterpark is one of three cable-run wake parks in all of North America, and it is quite amazing. It is, without exaggeration, an oasis. On one side of the park is a continuous pull system for wakeboard towing. A handle is given to you as you stand on a dock, and the cable latches and pulls you around a perfect manmade lake, complete with optional jumps, kicks, and rails. And if you're more into watching than doing, do grab a beverage from the snack bar and sit on the ample sandy beach. On the other side of Wake Island is another mammoth manmade lake, this one filled corner to corner with a custom-made *Wipeout* TV show-style obstacle course. It's fun, but more challenging than you think. You will be getting wet and loving it. The sessions on the course only last thirty minutes, but I challenge you to last even that long!

7633 Locust Rd., Pleasant Grove, 916-655-3900
wakeislandwaterpark.com

REALLY SOARING
OVER CALIFORNIA!

If you've ever been to Disney's California Adventure to ride Soarin' Over California, the virtual flying experience, then imagine doing that in reality! Blue Sky PPG is one of the most unique, most exciting, most glorious experiences you'll find in this book. A powered paragliding-certified instructor flies tandem with you over orchards and vineyards and through rivers and valleys in a fifteen- to forty-five-minute flight of a lifetime. It's not physically demanding, as the pilot does all the work. Powered paragliding is statistically one of the safest forms of sport aviation, and Blue Sky PPG is one of the best in the world. It is indeed a bucket-worthy experience. Take-off and landing is less than thirty minutes from downtown Sacramento.

1364 Sky Harbor Dr., Olivehurst, 530-308-3523
blueskyppg.com

OVERNIGHT
WITH AN ORANGUTAN!

This is the safest way to camp out within earshot of lions and tigers and monkeys, oh my! (Sorry, no bears.) The Sacramento Zoo offers special overnight camp-out opportunities that include dinner and breakfast the next morning. Speaking of dinner and breakfast, zoo ambassadors will let you tag along for nocturnal and breakfast feedings of the locals. You'll get private tours and campfire stories, fall asleep steps away from slumbering lions, and then wake to the sounds of calling flamingos. Don't know what they sound like? You will!

3930 West Land Park Dr., 916-808-5888
saczoo.org

PARTICIPATE
IN *THE* GREAT RACE!

Often billed as "the world's oldest triathlon," Eppie's Great Race has been on many a Sacramentan's bucket list for decades. This no-swim triathlon has participants run, bike, and then paddle in a kayak to the finish. Held along the scenic American River Parkway, the event attracts more than 2,000 participants each year in twenty-six divisions and is the largest paddling event in the continental United States. Participants come from all over the world, with the farthest competitor coming from Hong Kong in 2011. Ten days before the race, "Great Team Day" establishes timing for running, biking, and kayaking portions of the race. To do this, an Ironwoman, an Ironman, and a Team (consisting of local celebrities and corporate sponsor volunteers) race along the American River Parkway to establish the time to beat. Then on race day, participants beating these Great Team times win a complimentary breakfast at a local restaurant, not to mention the bragging rights to say, "I beat the Great Team Time." Can you do it? Just do it!

Along the American River Parkway, 916-480-0270
eppiesgreatrace.org

DANGLE PERILOUSLY UPSIDE DOWN
WHILE CLIMBING AN ARCH!

Yes, you can do that, although you won't really be in so much peril. At Sacramento Pipeworks, you'll find more than forty thousand square feet of climbing terrain and the largest indoor bouldering area on the West Coast. This is a great place for a date, as you'll need a climbing buddy to belay for you when you climb, and you'll do the same for him or her. What does that mean? Essentially, you'll climb in a harness attached to a safety rope, and the other end of that rope is harnessed to your buddy, who carefully tightens or loosens the rope as needed. It's much less complicated and much more fun than it sounds. If you've never climbed before, take the one-hour class and learn the basic skills needed to start! Back to that bouldering area: that's climbing without a rope; equally fun and safe, though a bit more challenging!

116 N 16th St., 916-341-0100
touchstoneclimbing.com/pipeworks

SUP SAC!

Sacramento has not one, but two lovely flowing rivers, and undoubtedly one of the best ways to enjoy them is SUPing . . . stand-up paddleboarding. If you've never tried it, now is your chance! It takes a moment to learn, but thanks to this well-run company, Flow Stand Up Paddle, visitors and locals can rent and get instruction on paddleboarding. The company also teaches SUP yoga and fitness and SUP race technique and even organizes SUP destination tours. It's a great way to spend an hour or a day, and it gives you some of the best views of the skyline as well as up-close encounters with indigenous creatures.

1501 Northgate Blvd., 916-599-6951
flowstanduppaddle.com

HIT GOLF BALLS
OFF A ROOFTOP!

Well, not exactly, though sort of . . . only better. It's hard to describe Topgolf, except to say, imagine being in a one-block-long, three-story restaurant, with the entire back wall ripped off, then being invited to compete by hitting balls out of that open space to targets in the lot below. Now imagine that your ball has a micro-sensor in it, so scores for you and your family and friends can be tracked on the hundreds of multimedia giant LCD panels around you. Did I mention that it's hard to describe? This venue is amazing; it's about twenty-three minutes from downtown Sacramento, but worth the drive. The food, beverages, and service are great, and the actual aforementioned point-scoring golf-like game is addictive. Good for pro golfers, non-golfers, five-to-105-year-olds alike. Be warned, this venue's sister property in Texas reports that people have moved nearby because of their passion for the product. Do this, and you may throw your other to-do-before-it's-all-over lists out the window. But not the window of this place; only golf balls are permitted to exit.

1700 Freedom Way, Roseville
topgolf.com/us/roseville

RUN
TO FEED THE HUNGRY

Having watched Run to Feed the Hungry grow from just around five hundred to more than twenty-five thousand people annually, this event is nearest and dearest to my heart. This Sacramento tradition since '94 is the largest Thanksgiving Day run in the country and directly benefits the Sacramento Food Bank. Join elite athletes from all over the world, as well as non-elite family and friends, all coming together for a great cause and a little calorie-burning before a lot of calorie consumption. The race weaves in and out of friendly neighborhoods. If it's your first time, it likely won't be your last.

J St., just west of the entrance to the Sacramento State campus
916-456-1980, runtofeedthehungry.com

RIDE
WITH THE WALKING ... DEAD

The Sacramento Zombie Train is a one-of-a-kind experience in which you and a hundred other people board a train, only to find out upon departing that you're riding with people who have "departed" in the permanent way. From October 2 to November 7, the Zombie Train offers excursions with zombie encounters on and off the train. It's a well-done mix of zombie fun, special effects, and theatrical interaction. The experience is family friendly; on my trip I witnessed a walker tone it down considerably when encountering a small child, and then turn the creep volume on full in another train car full of rowdy adults. There's food and beverages and a limited number of tickets available to be part of the action with your very own zombie makeover.

400 N Harbor Blvd., West Sacramento, 800-866-1690
sacramentorivertrain.com

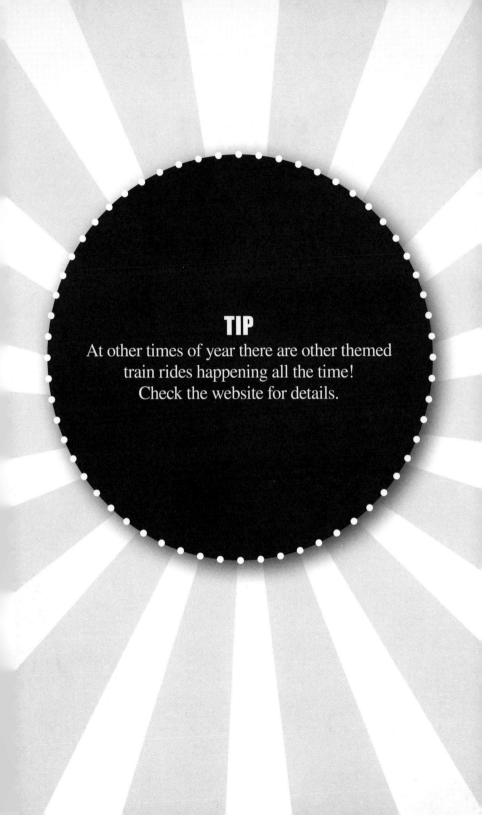

TIP

At other times of year there are other themed
train rides happening all the time!
Check the website for details.

SKYDIVE
INDOORS!

Why take the risk of jumping out of a perfectly good airplane when you can strap on a wing suit and jump into a wind tunnel to experience the same thrill! At iFLY Indoor Skydiving, training and flying takes about an hour and a half, and the actual flight is longer than the flight time of real skydiving. You'll get flight training, they'll gear you up with a helmet, flight suit, and goggles, and after the flight you'll get a commemorative personalized flight certificate to show your friends! Want a video of your flight? That's available too! Good for ages three to 103, and you need to be reasonably fit and healthy to participate; there are some weight and health restrictions, so check the website first. Then have a nice float!

118 Harding Blvd., Roseville, 916-836-4359
iflyworld.com/sacramento

SAIL AWAY

Learn to sail in only a day (or two)! The Sacramento State Aquatic Center is a great place to begin your pursuit of sailing. The two-day course will get you certified to rent boats on this gorgeous part of the American River known as Lake Natoma and will get you prepped for experiences on bigger boats and bigger bodies of water. Just want to get on the water for a floating picnic or leisurely paddle? They offer rentals of just about every personal watercraft you would want. Training takes place about fifteen miles east of the actual Sac State campus.

1901 Hazel Ave., Gold River, 916-278-2842
sacstateaquaticcenter.com

GET READY
FOR THE BOSTON MARATHON

. . . By starting with the California International Marathon! What humbly began in 1983 has become a world-class running event. It's a very fast point-to-point marathon, with a spectacular finish in front of the California State Capitol. It is certified and sanctioned by USATF and is a qualifier for both the Boston Marathon and the Olympic Marathon Trials. The race takes place in December, but entries are usually filled up by September. The California International Marathon is for the able, ready, and trained and is to be taken quite seriously. For the rest of us, feel free to goof around on the 2.62-mile maraFUNrun and Fitness Walk that happens concurrently.

916-737-2627
runcim.org

DANGLE OVER THE DELTA
ON A KITEBOARD

You may have seen thrill seekers zooming, jumping, and shredding on a wakeboard, apparently strapped by harness to a big kite. And you may have said, "I'd never do that." Well, never say never, because now you have reason to do so. Most locals don't even realize that for sixty to ninety days out of the year, the Sacramento area has the two key ingredients that make it a kiteboarding mecca: perfect fifteen-to-twenty-five-knot constant winds and an open body of water. Kiteboarders from all points of the globe often relocate here during this time, via toy haulers, campers, tents, or whatever in order to harness the perfect breeze. If you're ready to try it on, Nat Lincoln, a former world champion who lives in Hawaii and Mexico during perfect wind portions of the year, will teach you how to do it, from absolute beginner to being able to buy your own gear and enjoy the sport safely. His company, Edge Kiteboarding, opens and closes on Sherman Island each season with the wind, and you'll be able to track the dates online.

West Sherman Island Rd. on Sherman Island, Rio Vista
775-721-1132, edgekiteboarding.com

SWIM
LIKE A GOLD MEDALIST

Book a room and buy a day pass, or if you're the country-club type, buy a membership to Arden Hills Club And Spa! Since opening in 1954, athletes who have trained at Arden Hills have collectively set more than two hundred world and American records and earned thirty-one Olympic medals, including twenty-one gold, seven of which were won by legendary swimmer Mark Spitz. Mark Spitz swam in this pool, and you can too, if you have the means to do so (said in my finest Ferris Bueller tone). It is quite lovely, and I don't say "lovely" very often.

1220 Arden Hills Lane, 916-482-6111
ardenhills.club

LIVE A FAIRYTALE LIFESTYLE
FOR FREE

Sacramento has a park with giant artifacts from all the children's classic fairy tales. You know of "the old woman who lived in a shoe"? You'll find her house-sized shoe here. Humpty Dumpty's bridge? That's here too, and a lot more, with plenty of attractions, animals, gardens, and stages. They're open year-round, but once a year, on December 24, you can get into Fairytale Town for free! With the park decorated for the holidays, it's a wonderful way to spend Christmas Eve day, kids or no kids! If kids are a part of the plan, it's a great way to burn off the energy they have built up in excitement and anticipation for the big day!

3901 Land Park Dr., 916-808-5233
fairytaletown.org

JUMP OUT
OF A PERFECTLY GOOD AIRPLANE!

Okay, so this has been on the bucket list of just about everyone since the sport of skydiving was invented. The Sacramento area is home to the Parachute Center, a world-class training center, and in fact it is one of the oldest and largest drop zones in the nation. Did you see the squirrel suit stunt sequences in *Transformers* or *Point Break*? They trained for that here. So maybe you're not ready for that, but you'd like to jump out of a perfectly good airplane while strapped to someone who knows what they're doing? This is the place. It comes with risks, but so did the twenty-three-mile drive to get here, and you didn't sign a waiver for that, did you?

23597 N. Highway 99, Acampo, 209-369-1128
parachutecenter.com

HEAR SOMEONE SAY
"IF IT AIN'T RUBBIN' IT AIN'T RACIN' "
IN CONTEXT!

That is to say, see, hear, and feel the fury of a real NASCAR race live! The All American Speedway is a NASCAR-sanctioned track, and though they race year-round, make it your goal to see the NASCAR K&N West Championships every October at this track. It's a relatively small oval, and there's not a bad seat in the stands! Twenty-two minutes from downtown. Git 'er dun! (Start practicing your NASCAR-speak on the drive up).

800 All America City Blvd., Roseville, 916-786-2025
allamericanspeedway.com

EXPERIENCE
THE ROARING THRILL OF CLASS 2 RAFTING RAPIDS!

If you know anything about rafting, you know that "Class 2" isn't exactly roaring; in fact it's barely a ripple. But that's only ten seconds out of your three-and-a-half-hour lazy float down the American River. Most of it is self-guided, so you can just sit there and relax in your raft on your Class 1 journey. Though not challenging, it is a fun, potentially relaxing, potentially wild day—depending on how you do it. You can rent rafts for two to twelve people and even join several rafts together to form your own floating festival. Simply let the current take you while you picnic, or you can organize water cannon shootouts, races, or invent your own river ritual. American River Raft Rentals has been doing it the longest and will help you make the most of your day. Expect to carry a big, sturdy raft about one-quarter mile down a road, through a trail, and into the river. Fortunately, about three-and-a-half hours later (in my experience, right when you're ready to get out), you're at the correct time and place to get out, and you simply beach the raft and the company's crew does the rest. Then you'll wait a few minutes for a shuttle that takes you back to where you parked your car.

11257 S. Bridge St., Rancho Cordova, 888-338-7238
raftrentals.com

TIP

- To make it super-relaxing, get more raft than you need: Two people? Get a four-person raft. Six? Get the twelve.
- Wear sunscreen!
- Double zip-lock anything that shouldn't get wet, especially cell phones!
- Triple-secure your car keys because many get lost on the journey.
- Better to take more small ice chests than one big one.
- Take ample snacks, food, and beverages, but know that alcohol is banned on holiday weekends.
- On super-hot days, a sunbrella will be your friend!

BIKE
THE AMERICAN RIVER TRAIL

You could easily make this an entire day, or just a great hour. I did the latter, and only decades later found out that this glorious paved bike, run, walk, skate, crawl—okay, you get it—trail is thirty-two miles long! The American River Bike Trail (a.k.a. the Jedediah Smith Memorial Trail) hugs the banks of the American River as it flows through riparian habitat preserved by the American River Parkway. The trail runs from Discovery Park in Old Sacramento to Folsom Lake's southwestern banks at Beal's Point. The bike path meets the Sacramento Northern Bikeway just north of Del Paso Boulevard near Azteca Stadium. The two-lane trail is completely paved, with mile markers, trailside maps, water fountains, restrooms, and telephones along the way. There are also plenty of places to stop to eat, rest, or enjoy the scenery. Most of the American River Trail is shaded and level, although the route does traverse some rolling terrain. Along the way, you'll pass through several parks and swimming areas, as well as through the suburban enclaves of Sacramento.

114 J St., 877-448-1110
practicalcycle.com

NOTE

Don't panic, but be aware: about two miles of the trail is on-road in a designated bike lane, and parts are shared by many different users, including equestrians. There are places to rent bikes at several points; my favorite is Practical Cycle Transportation Company; they're also a great place to rent a bike for most of this book's offerings. All bike rentals include an optional helmet, lock, and handlebar bag. They will also expertly answer your American River Trail questions and guide you to the perfect hour . . . or day!

FIREWORKS
ON THE HORNBLOWER

Old Sacramento has the best Fourth of July fireworks, and the greatest way to see them is in the middle of the Sacramento River, complete with skyline, Tower Bridge, and the *Delta King* in your sights. Hornblower Riverboat excursions can be booked for parties, weddings, special events, or one-hour sightseeing year-round. And for the Fourth of July, it's worth it, although a hard ticket to get!

1206 Front St., 916-446-1185
hornblower.com

TAKE
THE URBAN QUEST!

One of the best, most unique ways to have fun in our great city and quickly fall in love with Sacramento is by playing Urban Adventure Quest, an app-based walking tour game. Grab some friends or family and divide into two teams (each with a fully charged smart phone), download the app, sign up, and get ready to go! I've never enjoyed Sacramento more, and in fact five items in this book came from discoveries on my Urban Adventure Quest! Each team is given simultaneous clues and cues to a walking tour of the city. It costs about fifty dollars per team, and each team can have up to five people. Your journey will take about two hours (not including any stops or food, beverage, or break times). Do it!

Starts at Capitol Ave. & 16th St. (the app will guide you), 805-603-5620
urbanadventurequest.com

JET SKI
FOLSOM LAKE

While there is nothing unique to jet skiing on a lake, within a very short time of experiencing a one hundred-plus-degree day in Sacramento, you'll be one hundred percent into it! The hotter it gets, the more perfectly temperate Lake Folsom becomes. And there's no better way to have fun in our blue Northern California jewel than by borrowing someone else's jet ski. I've tried not to name-drop excessively on this list, but the one and only time I rented at Granite Bay Rentals, Eddie Murphy and his family (who at the time lived a mile away from this beach) were doing the same. Prices are about what you'd pay anywhere, at any resort, for hourly and day rentals.

Granite Bay boat launch at Folsom Lake, 916-910-5335
granitebaypwcrentals.com

DON'T SCREAM
ON THE SCREAMER!

The story of this ride is almost, but not quite, as fun as the ride itself. It opened at Scandia in 2008, and within weeks, a city ordinance was passed making it illegal for anyone to scream on The Sky Screamer. It turns out that whisking people at fifty-five miles an hour 155 feet into the air and then hurtling them over the freeway and toward the ground (repeatedly) would induce a bit of a noise disturbance to local neighbors. Most people comply, and no scream arrests have been reported. Before or after you hold your screams, enjoy the mini-rollercoaster, mini-golf, batting cages, bumper boats, and hundreds of arcade options.

5070 Hillsdale Blvd., 916-331-5757
scandiafun.com

SKATE OR DIE,
BEFORE YOU DIE

Take a skateboarding lesson or just come to watch some of the nation's best skateboarding at 28th & B Skate Park, an amazing city-run indoor skateboarding park. Omar Salazar, former world champion, and one of the more famous skateboarders from Sacramento, inaugurated this ten-thousand-square-foot skateboard hangar. Three bucks to use the facility, but well worth it. Pad and helmet rentals are only one dollar. Dude! Do it!!

20 28th St., 916-494-8724
cityofsacramento.org/28andB

SEE
THE BUG RACES!

Sacramento has a long tradition of motorsports. In fact, in his youth, George Lucas once raced a car at Sacramento Raceway Park. But nothing here is quite as unique as the bi-annual (spring and fall) Bugorama, the nation's largest and longest-running VW event. Thousands of people and hundreds of Volkswagen bugs from all over the world arrive to showcase, race, and worship the mighty Beetle.

5305 Excelsior Rd., 800-929-0077
bugorama.com

CULTURE AND HISTORY

SCHMOOZE
WITH POLITICIANS

Did you know that you can walk right in and visit your local representative (if you're a Californian) at the State Capitol? That is one of several reasons to visit! At the California State Capitol, the past, present, and future of California interact with equal force. The building serves as both a museum and the state's working seat of government. Visitors to the Capitol can experience California's rich history and witness the making of future history through the modern lawmaking process.

1315 10th St., 916-324-0333
capitolmuseum.ca.gov

TIPS

Visit the gift shop in the basement, and get your shoes shined at the lower south exit. You'll likely be getting the same shine that many a senator and three United States presidents received. Also, although it takes time, negotiation, and a screening process, there are limited tours of the actual dome itself—a truly once-in-a-lifetime experience.

GO OFF THE RAILS
IN A CRAZY TRAIN ... MUSEUM

You might think you have an idea of what a train museum might be like, until you step into rail history at the California State Railroad Museum, spread across one hundred thousand square feet in six buildings. Until you've stared grill to grill with a 120-plus-ton locomotive, you have no real appreciation for the awesome industrial proportion and magnitude of these giant vehicles. You'll find several of those beasts, with just about every other kind of train in the history of rail transportation. There's a twenty-minute movie that gets you up to speed, and you'll meet some of the finest, most committed docents you'll ever find, dare I say, at any museum.

125 I St., 916-445-7387
csrmf.org

ROLL
BY THE REAGANS

While technically there are three houses you could see if presidential residential visits are on your bucket list, I'll skip #1 and #3, and here's why: Ronald Reagan only lived in the actual Governor's Mansion for a few months before Nancy orchestrated a move. She decided that the mansion would make a better museum than home. Plus, the twelve-thousand-square-foot home they were constructing in Carmichael didn't get finished in time. So the Reagans found a house in Sacramento's famous and exclusive Fab 40s neighborhood. There you'll find the cozy six-thousand-square-foot, six-bedroom/four-bath place they called home. It's on a lovely tree-lined and ungated street, ready for your photo op. But take your picture from the street or sidewalk; don't trespass or you'll wish you had secret service protection!

1341 45th St.

PARTY
IN THE MOVIE PALACE!

See, do, participate in *anything* at the Crest Theater, a grand 1912 vaudeville theater-turned-movie palace! The Crest was converted to its current glorious form in the 1950s and has remained untouched ever since. Take in a concert, comedian, or movie here and your experience will be elevated by the impressive history and vibe of this venue. Have a bite in the full-service Empress Tavern restaurant on site, named after this theater's historic original title.

1013 K St., 916-476-3356, 916-662-7694
crestsacramento.com, empresstavern.com

KILLER PHOTO OP

I'm sorry for putting this in, but not all history is pretty. At this location, you'll find an unassuming boarding house, once run by Dorothea Puente, a sweet little thing who looked a bit like Granny, the owner of Tweety bird in the old Looney Tunes cartoons. However, she had a habit of renting rooms to the elderly, stealing their Social Security checks, killing anyone who complained, and burying them in the back yard. This "I would have gotten away with it if not for you meddling kids" villain became known as the "Death House Landlady" after she dispatched nine of her tenants and used them as fertilizer by the time of her arrest. Technically speaking, a couple of them were used as a foundation for a paved patio. London has its Jack the Ripper tours, and you can see Lizzy Borden's place in Boston. Here in Sacramento, visit Dorothea's. I've seen people stop, jump out of a car, snap a selfie in front of this house, and move on. Super creepy. Don't block the current owner and don't linger too long. Especially not at night (insert maniacal laugh here).

1426 F St.

SEIZE THE TOWER

So, the legendary vinyl emporium Tower Records, the ground zero of the chain where "rock stars bought records," no longer exists. However, a slightly younger record shop has taken over its brick-and-mortar building in tribute: Dimple Records. And in keeping up with changing times, besides retailing vinyl music, they also rent and sell movies and games. The original Tower sign is preserved in the Golden 1 Center, and the theater named after the record palace remains Tower, with its iconic art-deco tower across the street. Russ Solomon started the chain in a store owned by his dad in 1960, and it became one of the world's most noted retail record brands. Join the vinyl re-revolution by picking up a classic disc at Dimple Records today!

2500 16th St., 916-441-2500
dimple.com

NOTE

Rent these first! The movie written and directed by former Sacramentan Tom Hanks, *That Thing You Do*, pays tribute to a small appliance store that ended up also selling records, and Tom's Sacramento native son Colin Hanks directed the critically acclaimed documentary *The Rise and Fall of Tower Records*.

DON'T TOUR
THE HISTORIC GOVERNOR'S MANSION

. . . Because California's governor is likely in there right now! The Governor's Mansion housed California governors from 1903 to 1967 and became open to the public as Governor's Mansion Public State Park by the 1970s. However, Governor Jerry Brown, who during his first two terms slept on a mattress in a small downtown apartment, decided to have the mansion renovated and restored to an official residence for himself and successive California governors. The mansion remains highly visible from the street, so at least stop by, take your pic, and say you were there. You won't see the $16,000 refrigerator that was part of the extreme kitchen makeover, nor will you see the 1902 Steinway piano that remains from the Pardee administration. But you will see a gorgeous three-story, thirty-room Second Empire-Italianate Victorian mansion that was built in 1887.

1526 H St.

NOTE

If your bucket list includes a photo of Governor Schwarzenegger's residence during his term, he lived in the penthouse of the Downtown Hyatt at 1209 L Street.

TRAVEL BACK IN TIME
IN A DELOREAN!

Well, at least see an original, genuine (non-movie prop) DeLorean, as well as hundreds of other amazing automobiles in the billion-dollar collection at the California Automobile Museum. Speaking of a billion dollars, did you know that Malcolm Forbes had a money-green Lamborghini Countach given to him as a gift? He evidently didn't need it and regifted it to this museum. The first car donated to the museum, a 1938 Buick Sedan, is on display along with plenty of other cool cars, trucks, and even RVs. Give yourself plenty of time to stroll the more than seventeen thousand square feet of automotive history. This is one of Sacramento's hidden gems, but hopefully not that hidden anymore after this publication!

2200 Front St., 916-442-6802
calautomuseum.org

JOIN
THE GREAT ART DEBATE!

Since 1967, Chicago has had a giant Afghan dog-meets-woman sculpture by Pablo Picasso on display, and to this day people stand around and debate why it should or should not occupy valuable real estate in the Windy City. The same is true of Jeff Koons' "Coloring Book No. 4," one of the most expensive art risks in Sacramento's history. This multi-million-dollar, eighteen-foot-tall hunk of cartoonish color and steel can be seen at the entrance of Golden 1 Center. Full disclosure: this author is friends with internationally recognized pop artist David Garibaldi, and I wanted his work here. Although I do love Koons' work, my thought is that "Coloring Book No. 4" would look lovely in Koons' hometown of York, Pennsylvania. But, that's the beauty of art—everybody sees things differently. Now go take a look for yourself, and then discuss!

Golden 1 Center, on 5th St. between J and L Sts.

TAKE SHELTER
IN SUTTER'S FORT!

History buff or not, visit Sutter's Fort State Historic Park and you will walk away knowing that you were in the oldest restored fort in the United States! In 1839, Swiss immigrant John Sutter received a land grant from the Mexican government and built an agricultural empire, which he named New Helvetia (New Switzerland). Right in the heart of Midtown Sacramento, this place takes you back to the pioneer spirit of families arriving in wagon trains during the California Gold Rush, a pivotal time and place in California history. Some areas are fully restored, while restoration projects in other areas of Sutter's Fort are ongoing. Committed docents in character are on hand for this mostly self-guided tour, and there are year-round special programs and events.

2701 L St., 916-445-4422
suttersfort.org

JUMP INTO
TONY STARK'S IRONMAN SUIT!

Technically speaking, you can't actually wear it, but you can at least see it at the California Museum. This is my favorite museum in town, and although it has many important historical displays, my favorite part is the California Hall of Fame, where every year a new class of inductees is added, all people born and raised in California, and artifacts related to each inductee are placed on the display. Robert Downey Jr. (thus the Ironman reference), along with Walt Disney, Joe Montana, Mark Zuckerberg, and a long list of other scientists, artists, entrepreneurs, and athletes who made the world a better place have displays here. The induction ceremony happens every year and is open to the public.

1020 O St., 916-653-7524
californiamuseum.org

SEE MILLIONS
OF MILLION-DOLLAR LIGHTS!

While Sacramento and its suburbs have dozens of amazing cooperative efforts from homeowners to create dazzling streets of holiday lights, the original must-see is The Fabulous 40s neighborhood. Streets numbered in the 40s in the Sacramento area are a collection of beautifully restored and renovated million-dollar-plus mansions. Think "original Beverly Hills," and replace the palms with oak trees. Each holiday season, residents in this area pay someone who pays someone to put up impressive displays. Some houses join together for extended displays; others light up individually, and they all crisscross the streets. It is majestic and not to be missed; see it at least once in your lifetime. Traffic gets heavy with cars, limos, even party bikes and horse-drawn wagons! Be patient, and if you only have time to see a few, make it 42nd to 45th Streets.

40th to 49th Sts., between H St. and Folsom Blvd.

GET A CONTACT HIGH
IN MEMORIAL AUDITORIUM

Don't worry, you won't, but for a very long time the myth persisted that so much "residue" from late 60s-era concert crowds lingered in the ceiling of this classic venue that you might get altered yourself just by breathing there. Opened in 1927 and remodeled in 1997 (with a thorough scrub of that ceiling), Memorial Auditorium remains one of the most recognizable and beloved buildings in the region and is listed on the National Register of Historic Places. Big bands and violin virtuosos opened the place, and the Beach Boys and Rolling Stones recorded here! See a concert or comedian, or rent the place out for a wedding or special event. Dubbed "Sacramento's Carnegie" by me, just now . . . but a well-deserved title!

1515 J St., 916-808-5291
sacramentomemorialauditorium.com

GO
UNDERGROUND

Sacramento founders got tired of having to repair and rebuild downtown every time the river overflowed, so they eventually built the town on top of the town, leaving the original largely intact in places below ground. Technically speaking, they "jacked up" much of the town in a process much more fun to see than to read about! Tour guides from the Sacramento History Museum will explain as you explore two spaces that were created by the city's successful raising process. This historical tour includes hollow sidewalks, sloped alleyways, and the underground spaces themselves. A colorful cast of guides ensures that no two tours are ever the same! Historical as well as specialty haunted tours are available.

101 I St., 916-808-7059
sachistorymuseum.org

88

GO TO CHURCH BEFORE YOU DIE, OR AFTER!

I said that mostly to tie into the theme of the book, which is never a bad idea. Do see, both inside and out, the Cathedral of the Blessed Sacrament, considered to be both a religious and a civic landmark. It is the largest of its kind west of the Mississippi, and because of its size, it has been used as the location for funeral services for former governors of California. Modeled after L'Église de la Sainte-Trinité (the Church of the Holy Trinity) in Paris, with a central bell tower rising 215 feet, this cathedral is a sight to behold. In fact, grab a table and have a cup of coffee across the street at Ambrosia Café for the best vista and street ambiance you'll have in this town. Though this is an active cathedral year-round, there is a gift shop, and tours can be booked on site.

1017 11th St., 916-444-3071
cathedralsacramento.org

SPEND THE NIGHT,
PERHAPS YOUR LAST,
IN THE PRESTON CASTLE

One look at Preston Castle and you'll shudder at the possibility of actually entering, let alone the idea of spending the night inside with real ghostbusters. One of the oldest and best-known reform schools in the United States, it opened in 1894, housing wards of the state transferred from San Quentin State Prison. Stories of horror and haunting, both real and myth, abound; you'll hear more about them once inside (insert evil laugh here). Vacated in 1960, little has been done to restore or de-creep the building, now an official California Historical Landmark, listed on the National Register of Historic Places. A must-see before you die, and perhaps after (insert another evil laugh here). Overnight haunted tours are best, and even better if on a Friday the 13th or Halloween!

900 Palm Dr., Ione, 209-256-3623
prestoncastle.com

BE A PART
OF THE SCANDAL,
OR SEVERAL

The Citizen Hotel is worth a visit or stay for a multitude of reasons. Construction began on this high-rise at about the same time as New York's Empire State Building in the 1920s and has some of the same architectural cues. However, The Citizen Hotel opened first and these days contains some of Sacramento's finest restaurants. Grange Restaurant & Bar here is always spectacular. Scandal is an informal bar area located in a loft right over the check-in desk. The motif is that of a law library, paying tribute to some of the early Sacramento law firms that began in this building. One entire wall is lined with autographs from famous guests who have signed a Scandal napkin. The fun here is to carefully look at the signatures and discover some famous people who in fact went on to have real-life scandals. I'm not revealing who they are here . . . go see for yourself!

926 J St., 916-447-2700
thecitizenhotel.com

GET NAKED
IN PUBLIC

I was trying to think of a clever, punnier way of saying it, but I opted to just call it what it is. If spending time at a nudist resort is something you need to get out of the way, here it is! Don't judge me; I had to try it on for size during a (heavily pixilated) live broadcast not too long ago, and honestly, the experience dissipated many of my preconceived ideas. As the Laguna del Sol clothing-optional resort says on its brochure, it has "members and guests of all ages, races, shapes, and sizes . . . a typical cross-section of the general public, with maybe just a little more willingness to try new and different experiences." We all spend a lot of time adjusting clothing; imagine not doing or having to think about that all day. Now, that's freedom! You'll drive about twenty-five minutes out of downtown for this special brand of freedom. This full-service resort has everything you would expect from a country club, including pools, spas, a fitness center, a lake, and overnight accommodations . . . all clothing optional. Here's a little tip: bring sunscreen, lots of sunscreen!

8683 Rawhide Lane, Wilton, 916-687-6550
lagunadelsol.com

GET YOURSELF ON LOCK
...IN LOCKE

Locke is a must-see stop on your Sacramento trip, located steps away from the Sacramento Delta. In 1971, Locke was added to the National Register of Historic Places by the Sacramento County Historical Society due to its unique status as the only town in the United States built exclusively by the Chinese for the Chinese. And what remains there today is truly remarkable and indescribable. It's not a tourist trap, and it's not a ghost town. Two blocks of the original settlement remain intact and unchanged. You'll find a boarding house museum and a gambling museum, both pointing to Locke's busy past. By the 1940s, restaurants, bakeries, herb shops, fish markets, gambling halls, boarding houses, brothels, grocery stores, a school, clothing stores, and the Star Theatre all lined the bustling streets. Visitors are welcome to Locke, and there are no fees for visiting. The entire town is a historical site, but it also is a living community; therefore respect the privacy of Locke's residents. And don't visit without stopping by Al's Place for lunch; you can't miss it, it's just about all that's open, and it's a remarkable family run bar/restaurant that continues to get rave reviews from the masses. It's the best in town . . . yes, the only one in town, but still very good!

Locke Visitors Center, 13936 Main St., Locke
916-776-1661, locketown.com

WORK
ON YOUR WARHOL!

While also hanging out in the longest continuously-operating art museum in the West. The Crocker Art Museum hosts one of the state's premier collections of Californian art, dating from the Gold Rush to the present day, a collection of master drawings, European paintings, one of the largest international ceramics collections in the United States as well as hosting tours of the most celebrated artists in the world, such as Toulouse-Lautre, Warhol, and more. They offer classes in art appreciation and hands-on painting and ceramic classes as well. The facility itself is a world-class destination; the original mansion, built in the 1800s, is now joined to 135,000 square feet of modern architectural wonder!

216 O St., 916-808-7000
crockerartmuseum.org

GO
BACK TO THE FUTURE!

Many movies and TV shows use the original downtown Sacramento, now known as "Old Sacramento," as a turnkey set for anything Old West, 1800s, or Gold Rush. The perfect time for the ultimate experience is during GOLD RUSH DAYS. Every Labor Day weekend the streets are covered in dirt, which brings the already original nineteenth-century buildings into complete "back in the day" illusion. Hundreds of actors in full costume and relentlessly in character parade around as gunslingers, robbers, gold diggers, snake oil salesmen, and pretty much every crusty character gold rush life would offer. River cruises, stagecoach rides, food, and fun!

Old Sacramento
sacramentogoldrushdays.com

SHOPPING AND FASHION

BE THE MASTER
OF YOUR OWN DISGUISE DOMAIN

Evangeline's is one of the best novelty gift shops you will ever set foot in anywhere, and it's also one of the nation's biggest year-round costume shops. You really need to go here to see true Sacramento history. Not many places can say they were once a brothel and at a later time a disco, in two different centuries. Evangeline's is in one of only four buildings to have survived the fire that destroyed much of downtown in 1852. It also survived its discotheque years to become what it is today. There is something absolutely silly for everyone among the endless isles of "stuff" downstairs, and two floors of The Costume Mansion above. Take the fully restored turn-of-the-twentieth-century elevator to the upper floors! Very Tower-of-Terror-esque.

113 K St., 916-443-2181
evangelines.com

BE FIRST
WITH FASHION

When little Julius Anapolsky arrived in Sacramento as a young boy in 1906 from czarist Russia, he had little more than the clothes on his back. Fast forward a bit to 1922, when he opened his store Julius with the motto "First With Fashion." If you recognize quality and true runway-ready fashion, and you have the means, then this is your place—find men's and women's fashions and service that would make Julia Roberts' *Pretty Woman* very satisfied. Once you're done shopping at Julius, stroll around the Pavilions, one of the nicer, more enjoyable shopping centers in the area. It's more Rodeo Drive than mall, it's outdoors, and when the weather is nice, there's not a better shopping, dining, and strolling experience in town.

580 Pavilions Lane, 916-929-0500
juliusclothing.net

HAVE THE BEST
CORN DOG EVER

They really have the biggest and best corn dog that you will ever eat. They're available year-round, and that's only one reason to make the twenty-mile drive to Denio's Farmers Market & Swap Meet. Founded in 1947 by Jim and Marilee Denio as "Denio's Roseville Farmers Market," by the 1960s Denio's became and remains the largest, cleanest, and most efficiently run farmers market, auction, and bazaar in California. From fresh corn to a reasonably priced one hundred terabyte external hard drive, you'll likely find it here. You'll find the bargains easily, but your biggest challenge will be deciding between the aforementioned corn dog and the Jimboy's Taco. My tip: stay long enough to have both.

1551 Vineyard Rd., Roseville, 916-782-2704
deniosmarket.com

BE KITSCHY!

If you've ever watched reruns of *Leave It to Beaver*, *The Dick Van Dyke Show*, or *The Brady Bunch* and thought, "I wish my living room looked like that!" then welcome to your mecca: M.A.R.K. Vintage. This place is two-thousand-plus square feet of all things mid-century, atomic, and otherwise retro (hence the name, Mid-century Atomic Retro Kitsch), located in an equally historic Sacramento art district. They also have kitsch-riffic men's and women's clothing and accessories. I once brought them a photo of a lime green rotary phone that I saw on *Mad Men*, and they found one for me. Yes, it's that cool, and they are that kind.

1021 R St., 916-947-2659
markvintage.com

PREPARE
FOR THE ZOMBIE APOCALYPSE!

I'm only saying that because a Cold War–era bomb shelter survival kit was my big find at the Sacramento Antique Faire, one of the top five largest antique vendor meet-ups in California. An outdoor Antiques & Collectibles Marketplace is held the second Sunday of every month, with three hundred vendors from all over the West Coast selling antique and vintage goods, such as furniture, clothing, jewelry, military (like Cold War–era bomb shelter survival kits), garden, architectural, lighting, and much more. Some of the area's best food trucks and vendors are also on hand, as you'll need to carb-load for the apocalypse!

2100 X St., 916-600-9770
sacantiquefaire.com

ARDEN FAIR

If you need to spend time in a mall before you die, Arden Fair is the nicest, closest, and oldest; it opened in 1957. If you can't find what you're looking for in the 1,108,852 square feet of shops, you likely don't need it before you die. The typical must-be-in-a-mall shops like Apple, Macy's, and the city's first Nordstrom are all right here. If that's not enough, you're only eighty-four medium-gaited steps away from another very nice shopping center, the Market Square, where you can grab some sushi at my friend Taro's place, aptly named . . . Taro's!

1689 Arden Way, 916-920-1167
ardenfair.com

SUGGESTED
ITINERARIES

DATE NIGHT

SPORTS & GAME FANS

MUSIC FANS

FUN WITH THE KIDS

LET'S DO IT OUTSIDE

OFF THE BEATEN PATH

INDEX

• •

• •

• •

• •

• •

• •